THE APPRAISALS POCKETBOOK

By Frank Scott-Lenr

Drawings by Alan Roe

"This publication is a concise but excellent reference book for all managers who are concerned with improving the performance of their people."
Pat Lunny, Group Director - Human Resources, Greencore Group.

"This pocketbook succeeds, in the clearest of terms, in demonstrating how to maximise the potential of human resources while focusing on the success of the organisation."
Pat Comerford, Director of Operations, Chilled Foods, Glanbia Foods.

"The Appraisals Pocketbook details a simple but effective approach to performance management - its models, forms and examples are most helpful."
Donal O'Connor, Director of Human Resources, Van den Bergh Foods.

Published by:
Management Pocketbooks Ltd
14 East Street, Alresford, Hants SO24 9EE, U.K.
Tel: +44 (0)1962 735573 Fax: +44 (0)1962 733637
E-mail: pocketbks@aol.com
Web: www.pocketbook.co.uk

Reprinted 1996, 1998, 2000

ISBN: 1 870471 29 6

British Library Cataloguing-in-Publication Data – A catalogue record for this book
is available from the British Library.

Printed in the U.K.

CONTENTS

AUTHOR'S NOTE

Performance management - the task of optimising individual and organisational performance - will not just happen; it has to be systematically managed.

This Pocketbook clearly shows how performance appraisal can be the vehicle for improving performance and enhancing the growth of individuals.

Once Key Result Areas and goals are in place, regular review and performance discussions ensure that the appraisal system is kept well oiled.

INTRODUCTION

IMPROVING PERFORMANCE

Most organisations are being pressured for improved performance.
Managers are being asked to get more from less resources.

At the same time, employees in many organisations are asking for better and more direct feedback on their performance.

The performance of an organisation depends **directly** on the performance of its key people.

Most progressive organisations therefore have, or are implementing, a system of performance appraisal - most regularly a goals oriented system, as described in this Pocketbook.

IMPROVING PERFORMANCE

Improved performance will not just happen, it must be managed!

Helping managers and their subordinates to focus on priorities within their jobs is the first step to managing performance.

A performance appraisal system allows an individual manager to achieve clarity with his/her member of staff about their precise job, and the goals they should be achieving within it.

HIGH PERFORMANCE CULTURES

Organisations aspiring towards high performance cultures are strong on:

- Clarity about objectives and goals

- Continuous assessment of performance and feedback

- Recognition for performance

This is a basic part of the managerial function of all line managers. Optimum performance is best achieved by the above three steps.

THE GOALS ORIENTED APPROACH

It is usually a **motivating experience for employees** to see clearly achievable goals in front of them and to be recognised by management when they achieve these goals.

Performance Appraisal Model

**The goals oriented approach
outlined in this Pocketbook
is a 5 stage model
as follows:**

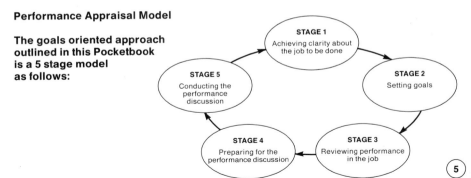

STAGE 1
Achieving clarity about
the job to be done

STAGE 2
Setting goals

STAGE 3
Reviewing performance
in the job

STAGE 4
Preparing for the
performance discussion

STAGE 5
Conducting the
performance
discussion

INTRODUCTION

SUMMARY

- Performance must be managed

- High performance cultures are strong on:
  - objectives and goals
  - continuous assessment and feedback
  - recognition for performance

- Appraising performance is a core system within management

- A goals oriented approach focuses on **the job itself**

OBJECTIVES AND BENEFITS OF AN APPRAISAL SYSTEM

KEY OBJECTIVES

The overall objective of a performance appraisal system may differ from one organisation to another. Specific objectives will depend on the needs of the organisation at a particular time, but try not to have too many.

In general, any system of appraisal or review is likely to include two major objectives:

- **Improvement of individual performance**

- **Personal development of the employee**

KEY OBJECTIVES

1 Improving individual performance

- Management should not be afraid to state clearly that improving individual performance comes first
- Departmental and organisational performance should improve as a consequence

2 Personal development of employees

- Important - employees must be able to see some benefit to themselves from a performance appraisal system
- Adopting the personal development of the employee as a key objective will demonstrate this
- In which case, management must ensure delivery of this development

OBJECTIVES AND BENEFITS

KEY BENEFITS
DEEPER UNDERSTANDING OF THE JOB

- Very often managers and subordinates, always under pressure from lack of time, **do not fully understand the key elements of one another's jobs**

- A successfully operated performance appraisal system, along the lines described in this Pocketbook, greatly facilitates this understanding:
  - it instivutes direct dialogue on a regular basis
  - the focus is on the job itself, and
  - the performance of the individual within the job

KEY BENEFITS
FOCUS IS ON THE REAL NEEDS OF THE BUSINESS

- A key element within a performance appraisal system that is goals oriented is that it **focuses on the needs of the business** and not on esoteric values unrelated to pressures within the business

- This clearly benefits line managers, when organisational and/or departmental goals can be adapted to form part of an individual's goals

KEY BENEFITS
IMPROVED COMMUNICATIONS

In a busy, over-pressured working environment, managers frequently fail to allow time to communicate adequately with their staff.

A goals oriented system facilitates **communication about the really important issues concerning achievement in a particular job.**

Typically, the quality of this communication is better and deeper than normal day-to-day discussions.

OBJECTIVES AND BENEFITS

KEY BENEFITS
MANAGEMENT COMMITMENT

None of the benefits described will be fully realised unless **the senior management team takes a very active interest in the process of performance appraisal and management.** Their commitment to this is vital.

- Commitment is a set of behaviours

- Thus, managers must be seen to do things differently after the introduction of such a system

- You only know an individual is committed to a new process if you see them clearly behaving in a manner consistent with the new process

SUMMARY

Objectives

- Do not have too many objectives
- Objectives should include:
  - individual performance improvement
  - personal development

Benefits

Organisational benefits will include:

- Deeper understanding of the job
- Greater focus on real needs of the business
- Improved communication

Follow-up

The management team must fully commit themselves to all aspects of performance appraisal and management.

STAGE ONE
ACHIEIVING CLARITY ABOUT THE JOB TO BE DONE

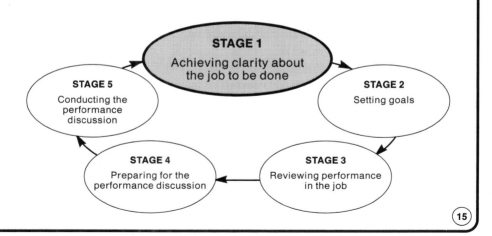

STAGE 1
Achieving clarity about the job to be done

STAGE 5
Conducting the performance discussion

STAGE 2
Setting goals

STAGE 4
Preparing for the performance discussion

STAGE 3
Reviewing performance in the job

JOB OBJECTIVE

The first stage in any system of performance appraisal must be to identify and understand:

- The job objective

- The Key Result Areas (KRAs)

This must be achieved before setting job goals of any sort.

CLARITY ABOUT THE JOB

JOB OBJECTIVE

Many managers take it for granted that the objective of a job is obvious and clearly understood, an unsafe assumption.

Try this test:

You and your subordinate sit down in separate rooms and each write down the job objective for both of your jobs.

The resulting misunderstandings may surprise you.

Clarifying the job objective also clarifies the context for Key Result Areas and goal setting.

CLARITY ABOUT THE JOB

KEY RESULT AREAS

Key Result Areas are those aspects of a job in which it is critical to achieve success, if the overall job objective is to be achieved.

Key Result Areas:
- identify the vital elements of the job
- contribute to effectiveness - by helping us 'to do the right things'
- focus on results rather than activities

- Manager and subordinate should together identify all the Key Result Areas for the job in question

- In most management jobs these will number between six and ten

CLARITY ABOUT THE JOB

KEY RESULT AREAS
EXAMPLES

Output	Technical Knowledge	Career Development
Customer Service	Product Development	Time Management
Sales	Delegation	Profitability
Quality	Business Development	Teamwork
Budget	Performance Management	Personal Development

It is difficult to conceive of any managerial job that does not have the Key Result Areas of quality, performance management and teamwork.

CLARITY ABOUT THE JOB

FOCUS ON KEY VALUES

Senior management teams may use the performance appraisal system to spread through the organisation values that are deemed important at any point in time.

For example, Key Result Areas could be established for all managers in any one area of customer service, total quality or productivity/efficiency.

Use the **performance appraisal system to reinforce other important programmes or emphases in your organisation**.

CLARITY ABOUT THE JOB

SUMMARY

Job Objectives

- Job objectives clarify the context for goal setting

- Managers often take it for granted that their subordinates are clear about their job objective

Key Result Areas

- Those aspects of a job that are critical for attaining the job objective

- Establishing Key Result Areas helps effectiveness

- Key Result Areas are a further step towards enhanced clarity

- KRAs can help focus the organisation on key values

NOTES

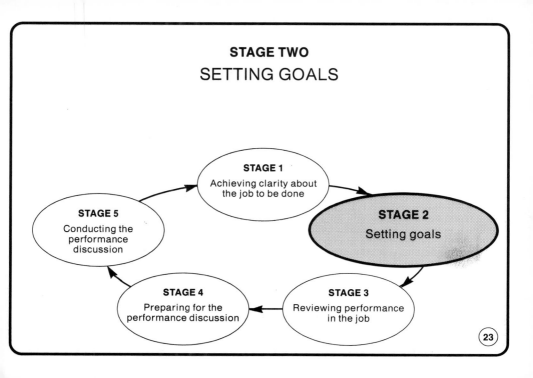

STAGE TWO
SETTING GOALS

STAGE 1
Achieving clarity about
the job to be done

STAGE 5
Conducting the
performance
discussion

STAGE 2
Setting goals

STAGE 4
Preparing for the
performance discussion

STAGE 3
Reviewing performance
in the job

23

SETTING GOALS

WHAT IS GOAL SETTING?

- Agreeing the job objective establishes **WHY** a job is done

- Identifying Key Result Areas establishes **WHAT** has to be done

- Goal or objective setting further establishes **WHAT** has to be done and begins to look also at **HOW**

Skilful goal setting focuses attention on the important targets to be achieved within each Key Result Area.

This helps employees to see clearly what they should be focusing on, in the period ahead.

WHO DOES THE GOAL SETTING?

- Goal setting is a joint exercise carried out between the reviewer and the employee being reviewed; goals are not handed down as tablets of stone by an aloof manager

- The whole thrust of a goals oriented performance management system will wither and die if managers do not fully involve their subordinates in this goal setting exercise

- Following goal setting, both parties should be clear about what is expected of the job incumbent

- These goals can then be the basis on which performance will be assessed at the end of the review period

QUALITIES OF GOALS

To be useful during and at the end of the review period, goals should be:

- Specific and measurable

- Achievable

- Challenging and stretching

- Jointly agreed

SPECIFIC AND MEASURABLE

Goals must not be couched in vague terms. If they are to be useful at the point of performance, then they must be as measurable as possible. This is done by making these goals as quantifiable as possible.

The measurement of goals is improved by being **quite specific** and also by **using a timeframe** within which the goal must be achieved.

Failure to make the goals as specific as possible will render them useless at appraisal time.

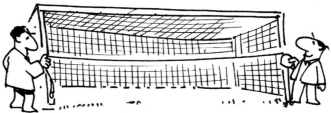

SETTING GOALS

EXAMPLES

Poor Goals
Improve sales in the company

Good Goals
Increase sales turnover in our sales outlets by 5% over the next nine months

Improve Industrial Relations in the department

Reduce by 25% the number of occasions when grievances go for resolution to the level above the first line manager; reduce by 25% the total number of grievances within the department

SETTING GOALS

ACHIEVABLE

Goals that are agreed with subordinates should be achievable.

- If an employee perceives a goal as unattainable then they may well become demotivated

- When agreeing goals with subordinates, take great care that both parties see the goals as attainable

CHALLENGING AND STRETCHING

There is little point in agreeing with an employee goals that do not challenge them, or stretch them to further improved performance.

As the reviewing manager, therefore, you must ensure:

- **That the goals being set are a challenge to the individual**

- **That they also stretch what already may be very good performance**

The manager should look for a little extra without bringing the employee to breaking point.

JOINTLY AGREED

It is important that goals are jointly agreed.

- Individuals will feel far greater ownership of goals when they have played a part in setting them

- This greatly facilitates their commitment to enhanced achievement

There may be occasions when a manager must, to some degree, impose a goal, for example when they are unable to bring the employee to the desired level of enhanced performance.

However, managers should be able to achieve the required jointness of approach in the vast majority of situations. Inability to do so, in even a significant minority of occasions, would indicate a lack of skill in the manager.

THE SKILL OF GOAL SETTING

Two factors make goal setting difficult for managers.

- A lack of previous experience

- Failure to take a structured approach

Managers can set better goals by providing each goal with **a structure that gives the goal a beginning, middle and end**. Examples of this simple structure are shown opposite.

As can be seen, the period for which the goals are set may vary. From one to four goals should be set in each Key Result Area.

STRUCTURE OF GOALS

BEGINNING Use an active verb	MIDDLE State what is to be achieved	END End with a measure (eg: quantity, quality or time)
Reduce	manufacturing costs	by 7.5% over previous year
Delegate	all analyses of quality reports	before end of 1st quarter
Increase	sales to blue chip companies	by 15% over previous year
Review	development needs of direct reports	prior to end of next quarter
Broaden	sales base of the company	by adding 5 new customers each month

SETTING GOALS

SUMMARY

- Goals are the criteria by which performance will be evaluated

- Agreed goals become the standards for performance

- Correctly written goals should embody the following qualities:
  - specific and measurable
  - achievable
  - challenging and stretching
  - jointly agreed

- Most managers need help with goal setting, through coaching and/or training

- Managers will improve their goal setting if they concentrate on always starting
  with an active verb and ending with some form of measure

STAGE THREE
REVIEWING PERFORMANCE IN THE JOB

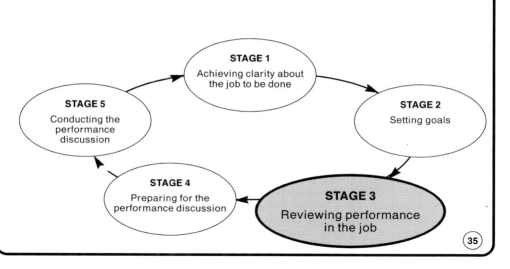

STAGE 1
Achieving clarity about the job to be done

STAGE 2
Setting goals

STAGE 3
Reviewing performance in the job

STAGE 4
Preparing for the performance discussion

STAGE 5
Conducting the performance discussion

(35)

CONTINUOUS PROCESS

Many organisations reduce performance appraisal to, at best, a once-a-year chore, where often a one-sided discussion takes place, supposedly focusing on performance over the previous year.

The task of reviewing performance is too important to leave to a once-a-year event; it must be a continuous process.

Reviewing performance on a regular basis is a sure way of securing the benefits earlier outlined for performance appraisal and management.

MOTIVATION

Regular appraisal or review of performance has a beneficial effect on employee motivation.

- People who are accustomed to regular reviews and feedback will usually be better motivated

- The organisation develops **an achievement culture**

REGULAR REVIEW OF GOALS

In a dynamic organisation the **goals themselves may well need to be modified during the review period**. Events within the company or in the external environment may require that this be done.

For example, within the financial services sector, a shift in interest rates could radically alter the attainability of a particular goal.

- Without regular review, you risk approaching the year end with outdated goals

- This makes accurate assessment of performance impossible

REVIEWING PERFORMANCE

AVOID 'FORMOLOGY'

Many attempts at performance appraisal fail on the basis of placing too much emphasis on the forms that go with it.

Be warned: the boredom that goes with 'Oh no, not another form' is infectious - it transmits from manager to employee.

The more organisations can reduce emphasis on the 'formology' of their review systems, the better will be the focus on the individual's job.

It should, in fact, be possible to complete the framework for performance appraisal using a blank page. An example of a relatively simple form is shown overleaf.

REVIEWING PERFORMANCE

SAMPLE FORM

PERFORMANCE REVIEW

NAME: _____ JOB TITLE: _____ DATE: _____

JOB OBJECTIVE/PURPOSE: _____

KEY RESULT AREAS	GOALS			PROGRESS/ NON-PROGRESS ATTAINMENT/ NON-ATTAINMENT
	Beginning (Active Verb)	**Middle** (What it is you want achieved)	**End** (Measure)	

REVIEWING PERFORMANCE

SAMPLE FORM

KEY RESULT AREAS	GOALS			PROGRESS/ NON-PROGRESS ATTAINMENT/ NON-ATTAINMENT
	Beginning (Active Verb)	**Middle** (What it is you want achieved)	**End** (Measure)	

AGREED DEVELOPMENT/TRAINING NEEDS

ADDITIONAL COMMENTS

Signature:_____   Signature _____   Date:_____
    (Reviewee)   (Reveiwer)

AGAINST GOALS

The performance of individuals should be reviewed against the goals which you set earlier in the process.

This ensures that **performance will be evaluated against the criteria for success** within a particular job.

Find out, before you begin, whether any external issues or events have affected the likelihood of the goals being achieved.

REVIEWING PERFORMANCE

SELF-ASSESSMENT

The evaluation of performance should not be undertaken by the manager alone.

It is consistent with best practice in industry and commerce that the **reviewee is also asked to form a judgement as to how he/she believes they have performed during the previous year.**

This, in fact, is a maturing process for the person concerned.

- Give a copy of the KRAs and goals to the appraisee a few days in advance of the appraisal

- Ask the appraisee to prepare an outline view of their performance in advance of the discussion

GIVE IMMEDIATE FEEDBACK
QUICK RESPONSE AFTER INCIDENTS

Many people can remember being told at appraisal time of 'incidents' that had, in fact, taken place several weeks/months earlier.

Feedback should be given as close as possible to the event, rather than stored up for some rainy day.

This achieves maximum benefit in situations where:

● Change is required in the event of poor performance

● Positive reinforcement is required for good performance

Such continuous feedback will ensure that there are no surprises at the end of the review period.

REVIEWING PERFORMANCE

SUMMARY

- Must be **a continuous process**

- Regular reviewing of performance **motivates employees**

- **Reduce** emphasis **on forms**

- Review performance **against goals**

- **Encourage self-assessment**

- Value the **feedback process**

NOTES

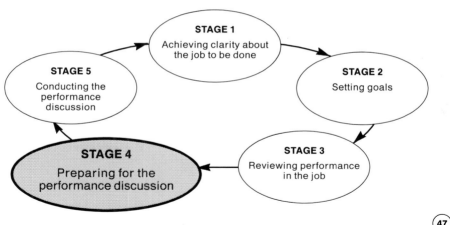

STAGE FOUR
PREPARING FOR THE PERFORMANCE DISCUSSION

STAGE 1
Achieving clarity about the job to be done

STAGE 2
Setting goals

STAGE 3
Reviewing performance in the job

STAGE 4
Preparing for the performance discussion

STAGE 5
Conducting the performance discussion

47

PREPARING FOR THE DISCUSSION

CHECKLIST

To prepare satisfactorily for a performance discussion, managers must consider:

- Assessing the **individual's performance** in the job

- Preparing the **structure** of the discussion

- Preparing the **reviewee** prior to the meeting

- Helping the **reviewee** to understand the system

- Developing skills for the **reviewee**

- Planning for good **use of time**

- **Job focus** - not 'systems' focus

PREPARING FOR THE DISCUSSION

ASSESSING INDIVIDUAL PERFORMANCE

The first stage in your preparation: examine performance in the job.

● Are the existing Key Result Areas and goals still relevant?

● Have the goals set for the year been achieved?

● If not, were the reasons **within** the individual's control?

● What specific behaviours hindered or facilitated attainment of the goals?
(Knowing this will help with the exchanges during the discussion)

Make sure that the review is in the context of the **whole year**, not just focused on recent events.

PREPARING FOR THE DISCUSSION

PLAN THE STRUCTURE

- It will be helpful to **prepare an overall plan of how time will be used during the discussion;** this permits you to emphasise one issue over another by ensuring, through your plan, that this issue gets more time

- You should also **plan for the specific ways in which you will involve the reviewee;** an appraisal is supposed to be a two-way process - it is all too easy for the reviewer to spend far too much time talking

A structure some find helpful is to plan the appraisal discussion so that it has a beginning, a middle and an end. A sample preparation outline using this approach is shown on the following pages.

PREPARING FOR THE DISCUSSION

STRUCTURE
BEGINNING

- Opening - establish rapport

- Give overview of performance management system

- Give overview of process for this discussion emphasising
  - jointness, and
  - request feedback on own performance

- Request reviewee's view of their own overall performance

PREPARING FOR THE DISCUSSION

STRUCTURE
MIDDLE

KEY RESULT AREA	SPECIFIC WAYS TO INVOLVE REVIEWEE
Production/Service Output	
....	....
....	....
Quality	
....	....
....	....
Teamwork	
....	....
....	....
Customer Service	
....	....
....	....

At the end of discussion **on each KRA,** summarise briefly and refer to next year's goals

PREPARING FOR THE DISCUSSION

STRUCTURE
MIDDLE: EXAMPLE

KEY RESULT AREA	SPECIFIC WAYS TO INVOLVE REVIEWEE
Production/Service Output	
Units manufactured in 1st quarter were 7% up on previous year	How achieved? Can growth be maintained?
Quality	
Cost of quality increased by 6% over previous quarter	Rework costs? Plans for getting it right first time?
Teamwork	
Team pulling together much better this year	How did you improve team spirit?
Customer Service	
No. of customer complaints on two of our designs increased by 14%	Why? Warning signs missed? What corrective action taken?

At the end of discussion **on each KRA,** summarise briefly and refer to next year's goals

STRUCTURE
END

- Overall summary

- Request for feedback to reviewer on ways that he/she may be helping/hindering performance

- Thanks!

PREPARING FOR THE DISCUSSION

REVIEWEE SHOULD PREPARE

A successful appraisal system relies on reviewee involvement and two-way discussion.

To achieve this, the reviewee needs to have spent time preparing for the interview.

Encourage the individual:

- To review his/her performance against the agreed goals

- To produce data on which performance will be reviewed

Good preparation will pave the way for detailed discussion which focuses on the job done.

PREPARING FOR THE DISCUSSION

HELP FOR REVIEWEE

Many organisations approach performance appraisal without providing any help for employees on how they should cope with the overall system and, in particular, with the performance discussion.

It greatly facilitates the smooth running of performance discussions if adequate preparatory work is done.

Initially, such help can be provided by **clearly explaining the system's objectives, principal elements and values** to all staff who will be affected by the system.

PREPARING FOR THE DISCUSSION

SKILLS FOR REVIEWEE

If the reviewee feels defensive it is difficult to continue a constructive two-way performance discussion. It is worth arranging coaching in ways to **increase openness and to encourage individuals away from over defensive behaviour.** Such coaching can be undertaken by any line manager involving small groups of direct reports.

If the individual manager is capable of clearly demonstrating his/her own openness and ability to avoid becoming defensive in the face of feedback, the development of these skills in subordinates is greatly enhanced.

PREPARING FOR THE DISCUSSION

PLAN GOOD USE OF TIME

One aspect of preparation work is critical and requires detailed planning.

- You must have a **clear vision of the state of mind you want your subordinate to be in at the end of the discussion**

- You must plan the amounts of time you need to spend on separate parts of the discussion in order to achieve this state of mind

Failure to plan can lead you into the trap of spending too much time on one or two negative aspects within a generally positive performance. This leaves the employee with a very negative view of his/her overall performance, which may not have been your intention.

PREPARING FOR THE DISCUSSION

PLAN GOOD USE OF TIME
BEING CRITICAL

If adverse criticism needs making, do not be afraid of it. If handled correctly it can be of benefit to both manager and employee.

Three rules to follow:

1 Do not allow the negative aspects to monopolise all the airtime available

2 **The overall concentration of time for the discussion should, in the vast majority of cases, be on strengths and thereby highlight positive performance**

3 Plan to start and end on a positive note

PREPARING FOR THE DISCUSSION

FOCUS ON JOB NOT SALARY

Money is important to individuals and needs ultimately to be linked with performance management. **However, the discussion of performance should be separated from any discussion concerning salary by as much time as possible.**

This allows:

- Full concentration on job performance and what will enhance it

- No distraction for the appraisee of waiting to hear, at the end of the discussion, what adjustment will be made to their salary

- No clouding of a positive appraisal by pay gripes

Discussions concerning salary, when they take place later, will obviously have to refer to performance but the two discussions should be as separate in time as possible.

PREPARING FOR THE DISCUSSION

SUMMARY

- Assess performance against goals

- Be specific about what helped/hindered goal attainment

- Prepare an overall plan for the various components of the discussion

- Be specific about how you will involve the employee

- Prepare employees by coaching them to greater openness

- Visualise the state of mind you wish the employee to be in at the end of the discussion and plan accordingly

- Do not over-emphasise negatives; do allude to them when necessary

- Plan to separate in time as much as possible the performance discussion and the salary review discussion

NOTES

STAGE FIVE
CONDUCTING THE PERFORMANCE DISCUSSION

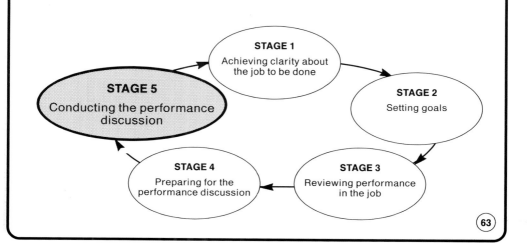

STAGE 5
Conducting the performance discussion

STAGE 1
Achieving clarity about the job to be done

STAGE 2
Setting goals

STAGE 3
Reviewing performance in the job

STAGE 4
Preparing for the performance discussion

ATTITUDE

We now come to the event that can make or break an appraisal system in one fell swoop: the face-to-face discussion between manager and subordinate.

- It is critical that the manager gives the discussion the attention it deserves

- Failure to treat the meeting with respect will deliver the clear message that the system itself is held in contempt, by you or even by the whole organisation

CONDUCTING THE DISCUSSION

PREPARATION

The most important element within appraisal discussions is the level of **preparation that is put into them.**

Building on the preparation model on pages 51-54, you need to **structure each interview at preparation stage** so that it is quite clear what will be happening at the beginning, middle and end of the discussion.

When using a blank page for this preparation, much of what goes into the box at the beginning and at the end will be reasonably similar from one interview to the next; it is the **middle portion that will require the major part of planning** for each separate discussion.

CONDUCTING THE DISCUSSION

MEETING ARRANGEMENTS

The manager is responsible for arranging:

- A suitable time during which there will be no interruptions

- Adequate advance notice of the meeting to allow the appraisee to prepare

- Cover for phone calls

- Understanding from all other staff/colleagues that no interruptions are acceptable

- A location that preferably will not require either party to sit behind a desk

- As relaxed an atmosphere as possible - consider the use of some ice-breakers

CONDUCTING THE DISCUSSION

FULL INVOLVEMENT OF REVIEWEE

It is critical that the person being reviewed **is involved and feels involved** in the performance appraisal discussion. A discussion is a **two-way** interchange!

The reviewing manager should be quite clear before starting the interview on the value of involving the employee, and plan specific issues/incidents on which he/she wants to hear the employee's view.

Failure to make performance review discussions a fully two-way process will greatly limit, if not totally eliminate, the benefits of such discussions.

CONDUCTING THE DISCUSSION

REVIEWEE'S EVALUATION

The appraisal discussion is not an opportunity for the manager alone to comment on the performance of the reviewee. It is an opportunity also for:

- The individual to evaluate their own performance, and

- The manager and reviewee to come to a common understanding of the level of performance during the period under review

A few days in advance of the discussion, give the individual the current copy of Key Result Areas and goals and ask him or her to 'pencil in' their view of their own performance. Once you have done likewise the **discussion can focus on merging these views.**

ACTIVE LISTENING

Most managers believe that they are good listeners. In fact, the evidence points in the opposite direction. This belief, on the part of managers, more often than not masks the necessity to improve listening skills.

Well honed listening skills are critical to appraisal discussions. Without them the reviewee will have the clear impression that the manager is not interested in his/her views; such a conclusion will again limit the benefits of a performance review.

Good listening is particularly important when the reviewee has evaluated his/her own performance more highly than has the reviewer. In such situations, the reviewer who listens well can usually better influence the reviewee to a more realistic view of performance, if that is necessary.

PROMOTE INDIVIDUAL DEVELOPMENT

A key objective for the system of performance appraisal is the personal development of employees.

Thus, due attention should be given in these discussions to **finding agreed ways in which the individual employee can be further developed. This will benefit both individual and organisation.**

Failure to deliver on this aspect of performance management, particularly if it has been a stated objective, will bring the system very quickly into disrepute.

CONDUCTING THE DISCUSSION

HONOUR COMMITMENTS

Managers often shoot themselves in the foot by not honouring commitments that they give during appraisal discussions.

If managers give a commitment on personal development or any other issue during the course of the appraisal, **it is imperative** that they ensure this is honoured in full.

Failure to do so seriously affects the personal relationship between reviewer and reviewee and, in addition, has negative kick-backs for the organisation.

CONDUCTING THE DISCUSSION

AGREE FUTURE GOALS

As well as reviewing past performance, appraisal discussions must also either **finalise or prepare the way for agreement on goals for the forthcoming period.**

It is possible to leave this aspect of performance review to a later session. However, it is advisable at the very least, as you conclude each Key Result Area, to outline fairly briefly what could be the goal for the forthcoming year and test how the reviewee responds to that.

This then leaves you in a position where it is a relatively quick exercise to dictate the future goals and pass them to the person for agreement.

DO NOT DISCUSS SALARY

Even though the performance appraisal system and the salary system must have consistent outcomes, it is of great importance that there be no discussion of salary during the appraisal discussion.

- The major requirement during the discussion is for the employee to focus on performance and how that may be improved

- If a salary increase is also going to be discussed at the end of the interview, then the **focus of their attention** will be on that **throughout** the discussion, **and not** on those elements of performance that can be improved

KEEP A RECORD

Successful appraisal systems are **about sharing thoughts concerning performance. They are not about filling in forms.** However, it is helpful to keep some limited notes and this can be done either on a blank page or on simple forms.

The appraisee should be given the opportunity to review any written record and comment on it.

Notes on forms such as shown earlier on pages 40 - 41 are only 'for the record'; the real emphasis is on the sharing of views.

FOLLOW-UP

To ensure that commitments are honoured and that performance is reviewed regularly, managers need to ensure adequate follow-up procedures.

This can be as simple as making a diary note to come back to issues that require a later response within a specific time period.

With such planning, you should get to the following review having completed all the items you had undertaken in the previous one.

CONDUCTING THE DISCUSSION

SUMMARY

- Full involvement of employee

- Get employee view of performance

- Active listening

- Promote individual development

- Honouring of commitments

- Agree future goals

- No discussion of salary

- Keep record of the discussion

- Follow-up

ESSENTIAL FEATURES
OF EFFECTIVE SYSTEMS

ESSENTIAL FEATURES

Continually improving performance won't just happen ... it has to be managed. Managed, that is, by the overall management team and also on a personal level by each manager.

It is essential that the following features of effective systems are incorporated into an organisational approach:

- Strong commitment from top management
- High level of subordinate participation
- Adequate organisational training provided
- Consistency of application
- Strong line commitment to regular recognition of good performance
- Outcomes from performance review consistent with reward systems

ESSENTIAL FEATURES

TOP MANAGEMENT COMMITMENT

- Top management must be fully committed to all elements of a performance appraisal system

- **Commitment is a set of behaviours, not just a memo or staff brochure showing support**

- One only knows if individuals are committed to something if they are behaving differently

- **Each manager, particularly senior management, must, therefore, question themselves about the specific behaviours that they will engage in to demonstrate commitment**

ESSENTIAL FEATURES

COMMITMENT BEHAVIOUR

'Commitment' behaviours required of top management are as follows:

- Promote the system actively, by regularly **talking formally and informally with people at all levels**

- Ensure that **performance management is a Key Result Area for each manager**

- Check regularly on the **manner in which the performance management system is being carried out by his/her subordinates**; more emphasis here should be placed on the quality of the reviews than whether or not they were completed on time

ESSENTIAL FEATURES

HIGH PARTICIPATION

Successful performance appraisal systems are highly participative.

Within a goals oriented system, all employees should be involved in the process of setting the goals for their future performance, and in reviewing that performance.

Many earlier systems failed on the issue of lack of subordinate participation.

The benefits that can be derived from such a high level of participation are:

- Increased reviewee commitment to the agreed goals

- Substantially improved communication between boss and subordinate

ESSENTIAL FEATURES

TRAINING

Many organisations introduce a performance management system without providing any training for managers who are to implement the system.

Without such training the system will almost certainly fail.

The specific skills required by managers are treated opposite.

SKILLS FOR MANAGERS

Two types of skill are required by managers. These skills can be very adequately developed in a short training course.

- The first is **goal setting**; experience shows that most managers do need help with setting goals which have the degree of clarity and measurability necessary

- Secondly, managers need coaching and counselling skills for the interactive side of performance review, to help with conducting the appraisal discussions

Undertaking this training also provides opportunity for overcoming some of the fears that managers might have concerning an appraisal system.

TRAINING REVIEWEES

Training for those who will be reviewed is often overlooked. These employees also have fears about the system. It is useful to conduct **a short workshop where employees can discuss the system and understand/develop some of the skills it will require.**

Such training could be described as the missing link for organisations who do almost everything right, but then leave out adequate communication and skill development.

Organisations that invest time in training their managers and employees reap the benefit during the implementation phase of a performance appraisal system.

ESSENTIAL FEATURES

BE CONSISTENT

Consistent application of a performance appraisal system across the organisation is a must. You cannot do without it.

- Failure to manage this adequately will result in discontented employees at various locations in the organisation

- Consistency is best achieved by making performance management a Key Result Area for all managers

- Senior management must keep a very close eye on the management of this, and check-up on one another to ensure consistency across departments

RECOGNISE GOOD PERFORMANCE

Good performance must be regularly recognised, although not necessarily in a monetary manner.

Managers in general do not take sufficient opportunity to celebrate or make a fuss about good achievement. We need to pay more attention to recognition, and regularly compliment employees where good performance is evident.

Managers who do this regularly derive all the benefits of having motivated staff.

ESSENTIAL FEATURES

CONSISTENT REWARD SYSTEMS

The performance management and reward systems must be linked, though separated in time.

In other words, **discussion about money should be separated from discussion about performance but the outcomes should be similar**: if you tell someone that their performance is very good, they should see a reflection of this in their salary.

It may take some time (up to a year or two) for an organisation to manage this linkage correctly. This is particularly so if the organisation is introducing a performance appraisal system for the first time. Appraisal skills have got to be mastered before approaching full integration with the salary system.

ESSENTIAL FEATURES

CONCLUSIONS

- A successfully operated system of performance appraisal is of benefit to both individuals and the organisations they work for

- Organisations intent on achieving success need to create a culture that will value achievement; an appraisal or review system that is results oriented helps to create and maintain such a culture

- Achievement of success in running such a system demands commitment and hard work by the management team

- Reviewing performance is a core system within management

- It brings about individual performance improvement and development of the individual

ESSENTIAL FEATURES

CONCLUSIONS

- The focus of the system must be on the real needs of the business and the individual's job

- For effectiveness, managers must concentrate on Key Result Areas

- Goals must be specific, measurable, attainable, stretching and jointly agreed

- Review of performance must be continuous, with regular feedback throughout the year

- Self-assessment of performance must be encouraged

- Detailed preparation by both parties is essential before the performance discussion

- Performance discussions are two-way communication processes

- Keep the performance discussion separate in time from any review of salary

NOTES

About the Author

Frank Scott-Lennon
Frank worked in manufacturing and service industry for a number
of years before joining the Irish Management Institute in 1980.
He is a graduate of the IMI/Trinity College Masters Degree
Programme in Organisation Behaviour.

He currently provides management development and
consultancy services in Ireland and the UK through his own
company, Quality Management Development Limited.
For additional information, contact his website:
www.quality-management-development.com

Frank has extensive experience of Performance Review systems as an operating
manager, as a consultant installing Review systems and as a trainer in helping
management teams develop their skills for the successful operation of Performance
Review systems.

ORDER FORM

Your details

Name ______________________________

Position ______________________________

Company ______________________________

Address ______________________________

____

____

Telephone ______________________________

Facsimile ______________________________

E-mail ______________________________

VAT No. (EC companies) ______________________________

Your Order Ref ______________________________

Please send me:

			No. copies
The	Appraisals	Pocketbook	
The		Pocketbook	
The		Pocketbook	
The		Pocketbook	
The		Pocketbook	

Order by Post

MANAGEMENT POCKETBOOKS LTD

14 EAST STREET ALRESFORD HAMPSHIRE SO24 9EE UK

Order by Phone, Fax or Internet

Telephone: +44 (0)1962 735573
Facsimile: +44 (0)1962 733637
E-mail: pocketbks@aol.com
Web: www.pocketbook.co.uk

MANAGEMENT POCKETBOOKS

Customers in USA should contact:

Stylus Publishing, LLC

22883 Quicksilver Drive, Sterling, VA 20166-2012
Telephone: 703 661 1581 or 800 232 0223
Facsimile: 703 661 1501 E-mail: styluspub@aol.com